ANIMAL SONGS

Poems by Dan Liberthson

Illustrated by
Cassandra Mettling-Davis

Cover design and layout by Joe Bui Art Direction
and Fish Tank Maintenance. Illustrations by
Cassandra Mettling-Davis.

ISBN: 978-0-9787683-2-4

To obtain additional copies of this book, please visit
Liberthson.com or major on-line book vendors.

Printed in the USA

Author's Note

Animals, both pets and wild, have been very important in my life and thought. They often see or sense what I cannot, and sometimes manage to communicate it. These poems explore the animals I have known both as creatures in their own right and as metaphors for or signposts to the human experience. I am grateful to them for enriching my life. I also thank the human animals who have helped with this book, in particular Judy Windt, Nancy Etchemendy, Custis Haynes, Kathy Rawlins, Joanne Whitney, Cassandra Mettling-Davis, Karen Wood, and Joe Bui.

Previously published in the *Haight-Ashbury Literary Journal* were Banana Slug, Dry Winter, and Birders and the Heart's Life. Twenty other poems have been published individually in *Miraloma Life*.

Contents

Part 1

Time Out of Mind

Evidence

There is a primal motion
of many merged as one
that makes my breath inspire
for it is nearer to divine
than any bush of fire.

Birds in a flock
whirl all together,
sweep across the sky—
no one seems to guide them
yet synchronous they fly.

Fish in a school
swerve as one,
each to the other tied—
by some means indivisible
they swim on side by side.

A herd of horses
swings around, thundering
full career
without a sideward glance
as if they feel no fear.

You tell me, mistrustingly,
raindrops swarming in the wind
shift side by side together
but this motion can be traced
to push and pull of weather.

No transcendent mind propels
raindrops or living creatures
through every curve as one:
coincidence and natural forces
conform that herd of horses.

Why then do swarming thoughts
that mix and shift like rain
arrange themselves in formal rows
all leading down and to the end
of making poetry, not prose?

These creatures move in unison
to laws instilled by prescient mind
above mere life and death,
sensed only in the sparking pause
of our indrawn, astonished breath.

Banana Slug

So bright yellow it seemed surreal—
kid's plastic trick, fat pepper slice.
Immobile, unknowing death or life,
on the damp path's shoulder it lay
amid twigs, leaf litter, and crumbled soil
split between hard sun, soft shade.

And I forgot it. Stepped past think-
ing this and that on the way to what
needed to be done. Until an hour
later I took that path again
and found it six inches
from where it lay then.

It's alive, I realized, and this time *saw*
the snub curved snout, sex sack
bulging at the neck, radiating antlers
reaching out, back ridge subtly
s-curved as it moved imperceptibly
to any briefly present being.

It was then I saw the trees growing.
Sensed the muscles in their limbs
bulk and twist as they made themselves
thicker, longer, through my watching
years. When I looked down again,
the slug was gone, and I had no idea
what time it was.

Taoist Tomb Tile

Radiant Queen Mother, Goddess of the West,
sails in her dragon-tiger boat
blessed with gracious retinue.
Sir Nine-Tailed Fox whisks away all cares
far to the East on salving winds.

Pharmacist Hare with great intelligent ears
holds his three-tiered retort high
and ushers to her lips easing potions,
while Milord Frog, Ambassador to the Moon,
strides potbellied, flourishing his scroll
and jaunty knees and smiling cheek to cheek
to ensure the Moon is fully pleased.

Four-legged Raven and bearded Guard with pike
stand ready to defend, but no threat comes.
The Tao has come: yin and yang are one.
Such harmony, such balance in the world—
Can anyone be frightened or disturbed?

In a Room on a Courtyard in Firenze

A giggling of girls swirls up, floats
lightly like a cloud of gnats
into and around the room and then
is gone out the window.

So cruelly mortal, sweetly immortal,
this sound pulls soul from body
as a trout leaps skyward
from a murky lake.

An instant mastering air,
it sees, miraculous fish,
a gyre of blackbirds turn
toward welling sunset,

feels cool air on wet skin,
and lives, this endless moment,
the whole of life everywhere,
with no fear of pain or death.

Re-entering, it becomes again
one with dense, obliviating water,
yet this blindness no longer
obscures all: the memory of seeing

reverberates like widening ripples
of girls' laughter, fading
yet captured in descent
by concentric circles,

insistent as the call
of a melted bell once flawless,
or a skeletal songbird perched
in past and future, present forever.

Lizard Story

It was a calm and tranquil day.

A lizard by the roadside basked in the sun
till my shadow touched his eye.

Frightened by the darkness,
he did push-ups
to scare the shade away:
it shifted, settled, stayed.

Off shot the lizard,
racing down the asphalt
headlong into a butterfly.
Too busy running, he lunged late.
Lunch flowered and flew away.

Lizard simmered down then
under new sunlight,
tilted his head to match his back's sway.
Into the picture a horsefly buzzed.
Lizard never noticed—too far away.

It was a calm and tranquil day.

The Octopus Pot

In Nauplion, city of myriad tiles,
the octopus pot dances in a museum corner,
dances for itself and the few who witness,
limbs of three invertebrates flowing
around its globe in womanly curves,
shaping since Minos' time the form
that holds all the water, all the earth,
every single thing singing through them.

A rumpled guard rests on the sill
smoking beneath the No Smoking sign
with no idea he would disperse
like his milky penumbra if not for
the embrace of three octopi
swaying in the sea encircling a pot
hollow but full of time and its children,
everything we are, and are not.

Flight

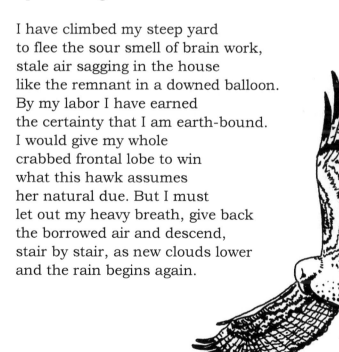

Days and days of rain past,
the clouds break open,
let through a shard of blue.
Just there, at eleven o'clock,
a hovering hawk slightly rocks
side to side, tail and wing feathers
feeling to hold the wind.
Suddenly, silently, celebrant he
stoops into a double barrel-roll
to thrill his close-trailing mate.
I am wracked with adoration—
my lungs try to draw in
the whole sky while she merely
tips her wings and steadies.

I have climbed my steep yard
to flee the sour smell of brain work,
stale air sagging in the house
like the remnant in a downed balloon.
By my labor I have earned
the certainty that I am earth-bound.
I would give my whole
crabbed frontal lobe to win
what this hawk assumes
her natural due. But I must
let out my heavy breath, give back
the borrowed air and descend,
stair by stair, as new clouds lower
and the rain begins again.

Birders and the Heart's Life

Those guys know all the names:
even when they can't see a bird
they listen for the call and then
jump and sing out in glee
wood-peewee or red-eyed vireo.
They make lists of every bird
they've ever met anywhere
and will draw you a picture
given half a chance.

So I went out and bought
the most damned expensive
pair of green field glasses
and spent half an hour caressing
the just-so texture the perfect
fit of the grips the green green
until Kathy finally said you're
supposed to look *through* them
silly.

OK, listen, here's some names:
ruby-throated thwarble
undulating crested calliope
purple-backed thwacker
haruspicating bittern
and I didn't even need
to see the damned birds—

but I hear them, oh yes
and I feel them
rustling through the underbrush

sailing around tight corners
back-flipping in wind twists
settling tight in their nests.

So I drag Kathy out of bed
five o'clock Saturday morning:
we're going birding! It's peak
raptor time at Hawk Hill
the paper says there's dozens
every hour and we're going
to see them all bring the book.
You're not a morning person, remember,
she says.

And the sun dyes the sky
whatever colors it pleases
and I lie back in the grass
paralyzed by beauty
and needing to pee
while two soaring Northern Harriers, wait
the color's wrong they must be
Swainson's hawks, yes, juveniles, no
wait they could be kestrels but—
the color, dear, changes every damned time
the birds swim elsewhere
on the wind: whenever the sun decides
that's enough here let's move up a notch
they become different birds.

But Jesus! Will you look how the updraft
curves their wings like lips
waiting for a kiss.

Part 2

To Love and Lose

Adoption

In the park a steady rain
thrums my black umbrella.
Turtles submerge in protest
but a snowy egret stands in a pond,
white against the gray sky, still
sounding, elegant fish listener
amid the rainwater bubbles.
Then my clumsy nearing
starts him up and off, long loose
head feather trailing,
pipestem legs wafting
through water-thick air.

He lands behind a treefern
ecstatic in the greening rain,
aware solely of its own spreading fronds
and tightly furled scrotum waiting
for sun to break open its knot,
uncurl its sex like a sprung spring
and with the first warm breeze
let loose its spores upon the air.

The whole natural world, guzzling wet,
awaits the onslaught of seed, the opening
burst of blossom and fresh life. But—
there, against a dumpster, a large fine
teddy bear sits glumly moistening,
dark eyes forlorn as a lost dog's.
What sort of mother would throw away
a child's long-treasured friend, what
father so crass, unless they'd lost all love
or hope, the child too discarded,
unborn, or dead. By the teddy's foot
swills a satisfied clump of buttercups.

A crow lands on the dumpster and directs
his appraising glance at the teddy.
The rain sharpens, takes aim.
The crow wheels, wet black flash,
and caws away to a drier place.
Silently the egret glides back to his pond.

Childless
I pick up the teddy and turn toward home.

Who Killed Cock Robin

The morning sang to itself,
soothed to robin's egg blue
a sky that had started gray.
Flowers opened their mouths
and uttered musical musk
while two butterflies twirled
in a blossoming lilac bush.

A robin strutted, note upon a line,
his breast puffed as he called
all the surrounding air his own.
Fourteen years apiece had not taught
my friend and me a way to honor this.
He dared, I aimed and pulled
and shot the robin with his pellet gun.

Fallen, he arched and threshed the grass
as if to fly through earth, not air.
I said *I don't believe it*, tasting bile.
What a shot! my friend replied.
We'd better put him out of misery.
He set the barrel to the bird's head
and shot Cock Robin dead.

The world in the yard skewed and I
emptied like a sieve, knowing at last,
clear as the blue glass sky,
that I and everyone I loved would die.
Nothing else changed. One birdsong
gone, that was all. Still in their bush,
the twin yellow butterflies twirled.

Mockingbird

On a post on the mountain a mockingbird,
with his bright barred back, calls and calls
in every language he has mastered, come here,
my pretty, come here. He flies up
a few feet and floats down, singing.

My dog can't grasp why I stay and stare.
He tries to haul me down the hill by force
back home to where his dinner waits.
The bird looks once, then ignores us both.
He flies up, dips down, flies up, dips down,
sings and sings and sings but no mate comes.

Lost Cat

My sweet black Nefertiti
killed by a car
thirty years ago
still sat on our windowsill
every dinner time
condensing from the dark
long enough to tear my heart
with one hooked claw,
then melt into the night.

Now another cat's gone missing.
Posters on nearly every pole
(as if sheer repetition could force
an answer to at least one prayer)
promise a THOUSAND dollars
for your return. Tabitha, for you
there is still hope (bait that keeps
love's teeth biting): your tabby body,
honey colored and dark striped,
has not been found. No bloody mess,
no fur tufts on the mountain
where some hungry raccoon
craved flesh more than cash.

Some comfort there, but shrinking
as the nights grow longer
and you go on missing.
Oh, Cheshire cat, you suckle
on our yearning more greedily,
draw love's milk harder
and make the ache sharper

now only your smile remains.
Without corpus delicti
we can doubt your death but
cannot trust your life.

If only love could do
everything we need it to,
but it cannot conquer all—
not even its own illusions.
Why must you return,
half ghost, to haunt our dreams,
when, waking, *here kitty*
draws only a phantom purr
and the faint wind sometimes
we think we feel stirring
from your ringed tail's passage.
As in heaven, we can't believe
yet can't bear to disbelieve.

Caribou

The immense racks of caribou
are living, feeling tissue early on,
covered with fine skin and fuzz,
sensitive to touch as an ear to screaming.
Later, they set into bone,
tear through the air
like a robust thornbush,
then shed in a single season.

The big bucks carry their racks
proud as any king wears a crown
and feel they must use them
as any king swings mace and sword
to cut pretenders down.
The does, circumspect, await the outcome
and appear not remotely concerned
when the males lock racks and starve.

End Games

1

Do you see that robin
batter his head
into the windowpane
over and over, convinced it is
an opening, not an illusion,
learning nothing
from a beaten skull,
finished for learning finally
by a broken neck?

This pathos evokes
a stubborn man,
like the man I am,
who will not change,
only brings more pain.
He cannot think he is wrong,
has been wrong his whole life.
To let in this doubt
would be to live
in a falling, driving terror
worse than any pain,
even from a broken neck.

This bird's compulsive motion
is like the loveless coupling
of a man in a cold rage
with a woman frozen by despair.
Battering, battering, head on,
he tries and tries again,
unwilling to give up
or she to let him through,
to penetrate the flat pane

to warmth sensed distantly,
a flame that gutters
the more he lurches in
and dies as he comes apart.

2

A man in a play in a dream is weeping.
Bird with a broken neck cupped
tenderly in narrow hands,
a slight young woman with
bright hair and corded arms
kneels before him.

Face pricked red
by anger's iron fork,
he hates the death
of this pretty thing.
"Why did you kill it?"
she accuses. Silently
he turns and exits stage right.
"What have I done?" she mourns.

He enters stage left,
walks to the bedroom window,
opens it and lifts the robin through
with both hands, which then clasp
as in prayer while the bird
drops without a motion.
A thud echoes across the stage.
The young, slender woman approaches,
but he has already closed the window.
Half turned away,
he does not see her facing him,

hands releasing a bird
that flies at the window and falls.
He walks on, does not turn.
The bird hits the window again.
Fade to black.

The Black Dog

Anything I think of hurts:
caught in this leghold trap
I can only circle
and circle back.

Once this leg's chewed off
will I at last be free?
Yes, but my leg will not
and pain will still hold me.

Two redtailed hawks soar
high above the trees,
being what I cannot.
They cry kree, kree.

---

*Perhaps borrowing from
Samuel Johnson, Winston
Churchill named his spells
of depression "The Black Dog."*

Missing Elephants

for Regina

You are gone now,
Callie, Lulu, Tinkerbelle,
who filled my eyes full.
But your absence,
even bigger than you,
is more present
than anything in this zoo.

You and your huge hearts
have moved to a paradise
like those we humans manage
near reservoirs, golf courses—
but yours is near tree courses,
grass courses, sky courses.

You are together
and you are free.
We are neither.

Dog is Love

The neighbor's beagle
locked in the garage
the whole day long
makes the most desolate
sound in the universe,
the wail of an abandoned soul
bricked into the walls of hell,
speared heart quivering
in an icy vacuum.

They have no clue
what it means to leave him
isolated, the worst horror
any dog or human could know,
how each day he dies all day
once a minute, forsaking sleep
and food for the truth of suffering.

They don't even have the sense
to be grateful that instead of
ripping out their throats
as would be just,
he licks their faces, wriggling
in ecstatic rebirth.

He's the opposite of us,
whose passion is for justice.
His is for love,
offered only by our kindest gods.

Angelique

A blaze of orange in a bowl of water
on a lap draws my gaze until
it becomes an ornamental goldfish,
fins waving like party favors
stuck on an upside-down body
assembled from misplaced bumps.

"She just can't stabilize," the lady says,
 righting her fish with a plump hand.
"Goldfish are bottom feeders, and she
can't find bottom so she's starving."

"What an amazing fish," I say lamely,
"what's it's name?"
"Angelique," smiles the owner,
"the sweetest creature you'll ever meet."
The fish nestles against her gently stroking hand
as if it knows the meaning of mother.

"The vet's tried everything,
special vitamins, antibiotics.
This is her last visit. I've grown
so fond of her, it will be hard."

My nearly paraplegic rabbit
slops in his box by the window,
hind legs too weak to hold him up,
sticks his snout and ears above the edge
and sends me his message of longing.

I go to rub his snout
as the assistant calls the fish lady
who smiles walking past
to the examination rooms.

"Such a nice bunny,
I hope he gets better."

The world is awash
with love for all its creatures,
not merely we humans.
This small, round lady,
ark borne upon the flood,
holds Angelique, a glowing lamp,
warm in the growing distance.

Part 3

Journeys

Gone West

Having sought in many places I've found,
far west, this rocky, fog-bound coast
and let it become home.
Heir to the ease and discontents

of one who has settled, I soak in peace
and regret (solemn duty of middle age)
lost raptures, shed husks of a creature
left behind, its meat no longer mine.

Now I'm as domestic as my dog,
his greatest joy the evening walk
and second best, back home to eat
and rest: the full bowl, the warm bed.

Yet he still insists we set out every day
to find the world and make it ours,
as if we've never come this way before,
may not again, and so must leave our mark.

A late October chill sharpens colors.
The last roses burn brightest of all,
red and yellow flares so intense
they spark my eyes to brimming.

In the dusk sky a frothy pink layer
barely holds up a steel blue anvil
crushing down across the horizon.
Urgently the dog pulls away, escapes

to root and riot by a hedgerow,
in his hermetic world of scent
immune to my seeping loss of sight.
I step aside and watch him come to life.

The great lung of night breathes out darkness.
Colors settle deeper, shapes dissolve.
Looking up, I lose my feet and fall into the sky,
nothing to grab hold of but the evening star.

A smiling crescent moon cups blackness.
My head spins with vertigo and fright:
the cup will tip and pour dark syrup down,
light and life submerge and all go out.

The dog finds me, leans solid against my leg.
I may hold the leash, but he's the guide,
the dolphin who will save this failing swimmer.
He knows the way, each day, out and back.

Canary

Orange flame in a cage
but absolutely free
in moments of motion,
he rocks on his swing
to and fro, side to side,
swaying in the unforced
wind of impulse,
smiling as a bird smiles,
in his entire posture,
with all the joy
of any child or dancer,
any live being
burning through its gift
of flesh, swinging up,
down, in life's cage.

A Shopping Experience

Sitting outside the "Amish" furniture store
somewhere on the back end of the Catskills
a grizzled woman smokes filters and looks away
from where I bide my time on a wooden barrel.
"Wife's inside," I venture, "I've got time to kill."

The woman shifts to look even farther away
but a gray cat with swirling chocolate markings
saunters to my side, wraps herself neatly
in plump tail, lifts her head and offers green eyes.
She accepts a stroke or two—
no matter that I'm from a strange coast.

"Scat!" cigarette woman hisses.
The cat leaps to a highboy on the porch,
then all the way to the roof in a great bound.
Padding up the slope, she glances back once,
neatly nods her head and then vanishes
elegantly and forever over the peak.

Cigarette woman's throat catches.
She rasps to clear it, but does not speak.
I watch the door. No one comes out.
Seldom have I felt so lonely.

Day Walk With Wife and Dog

At Stow Lake in Golden Gate Park
lesser scaup float genially amid
peddle-boating tourists in the uncommon
sun and our bird-dog eyes them greedily,
tightening the leash to twanging,
hungry not for food but sensation.

We've just learned of your cancer
and are here to compose ourselves.
We talk about the many times we'd
thought to rent a boat but never had,
the terrier our usual excuse: he'd freak
and dive in after the ducks.

I think how much you love birds
and how you opened my eyes
to those lovely feathered worlds,
and how, as we have no children, fitting
and terrible it would be if your bones
became hollow, like a bird's, and you

flew away while I was, as usual, dreaming.
What you are thinking? I don't know:
That all battles are won or lost?
Of the sweet turtles sunning on their rocks
and the comical dog seriously straining at them?
The vague warm air, the chill shadows, nothing?

Catskill Gnats

They bore in the more
you beat them down.
These unforgiving bugs
invade every crevice
every living space
until hands wildly
flail and smash
and mind imagines

conflagration

burning the round air
clean as fresh sheets,
cool and still as fjords.

But as heads severed
from the nimble hydra
replenish and thrive
or envy wells over
any containment wall
impervious to prayer,
force or subtle reason,
gnats remain, remain.

Dispute

In Chao Shao-an's bird painting
the eyes are most alive,
still points around which
nearly haphazard feathers
resign themselves to order
like a web of twigs
patterned by a streetlight.

On one azalea branch
several birds perching
all glance forward
(you can feel them!)
but one squawks sideways
(you can hear him!)
with a devilish glint.

Suspended on their branch
the flock
imminently will turn
to punish the disputant
or will ignore
his screams for attention—
but none makes a motion to fly.

Late Winter Outside Prescott, Arizona

A lake nurses a rim of snow
and slow ducks on its mild swell.
The silence is so pristine,
the unbroken snow so virginal
I cannot let things alone
but like a schoolboy loosed
pack a snowball and throw
at a bobbing ring-necked drake.
The shot falls short and the duck
unflustered in his gaudy colors
glances at me as if he knows
in Spring males of every species
cannot leave anything be.

Web

Early this Spring morning
after a night of bitter thoughts
that I have no love to give
I leave you
curled away at bed's edge
and let gravity drag me
slowly down the stairs.

Opening the back door,
I go into the stirring air
and stop short before the giant
washed web of an absent spider,
stretching from window sill
to lattice clear across the stairs,
holding at nearly every node
droplets of rain fallen in the night,
glittering now with new sunlight.

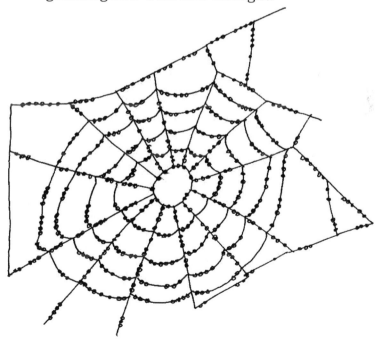

My dog surges up the stairs
but I am caught in backwash,
trapped in past time as if stung
and paralyzed by memories of childhood:
roasting spiders with a looking glass,
pulling off one leg at a time and
laughing at their lopsided sprawl,
all the while shuddering, fore-
knowing their brothers' revenge—
a blanket of spiders to cover me,
legs rasping, mouth parts reaching.

Yet they have never come.

I demand their justice but
not one will give me satisfaction.
The harshest punishment, they know
is to make me face myself,
paralyzed but still aware,
caught by this brilliant snare
and in the hard grip of beauty
made to remember
who I was
who I am
how far I have to go.

Part 4

Sauce for the Gander

Reply to Vegetarians

For soul's and body's sake
be vegetarian, I'm told,
purged of meat lust
till nothing remains
but milky kindness,
all creatures safe beside me.

But the lioness lopes home,
young gazelle clamped in her teeth
by well-broken neck,
wilted body swaying
as her cubs yelp in chorus,
saliva glistening on their chins.

And the hovering kestrel
drives down on an unwary mouse
who rushes holeward too late.
Beak blades shear her spine,
talons pierce her dangling body,
torn piecemeal for the chicks.

And the polar bear inches forward,
snowmound closing silently
on the ice-skimmed breathe-hole of a seal
living in discrete frozen beads of time
who notices nothing before, brighthot,
the lunge severs his red life-binding thread.

An opossum forehalf drapes
the stairs halfway up my yard.
Ruby rags remain where yesterday
hindquarters played, since mislaid
on midnight walkabout by our dog,
re-living the chase adoze on the deck.

He whines and twitches and I too dream
of lioness ranging, hawk gliding—
stalk the cunning hungry bear,
run fourlegged with wolves,
stretch out my neck for gobbets,
listen to my marrow hum.

Blood has always worshipped
blood. From deep in the throat
and far in the veins
a red, whistling tang
screams for blood,
hot unceasing rain.

Christmas Dinner

I bought an enormous goose
full fourteen pounds and more,
baked him to a luscious finish
and while our guests laughed
and chatted in the dining room
we fought in the kitchen:
I to force his final conversion
into parts to be rendered human,
the goose to hold the last of his wild
strange being, somehow to remain goose.

With sweat-stung eyes and fat-slicked hands
I wrestled him like Jacob his angel:
the flight-knit joints refused to part,
bone and sinew fought the knife
and the whole roasted body nearly soared
off the cutting board as once
the whole feathered bird clove the sky.

I stopped to breathe and in that moment
recognized the power of this dissevered
being, stubbornly persisting beyond life,
its rich and potent meat destined one day
to fly again long after our passing.

Carnivore's Remorse

It is the Paschal lamb,
the day after we ate it
for Passover dinner
and all agreed it tasted wonderfully
of rosemary, garlic, pepper, wine,
but here I hold the long femur
cold from the refrigerator, unbroken
and cradling hidden marrow
for which I lust.

The image of the table-saw
down in the dank garage
leaps into my mind's eye
alongside the legbone,
its meat gnawed off
to show straight white walls
rounded by knuckly ends.

And when the rip blade
severs it in half like butter
the odor is intimate—
of tooth burned by dental drill
and distantly (I've never smelt it)
burning corpse.
Each severed side holds
compact white marrow with blood
strands running through it.
I'd imagined roasted marrow, savory,
like the hip bone gnawed yesterday—
not this sickly white.

In the microwave, the marrow softens
and expands, crawling wormlike
from the bone's channel to the saucer,
partly melted yet holding shape,
like a large, hairless caterpillar.
I eat it. This half-bone's marrow
is bland and oily, mildly disgusting.
Unbelieving, I try the second half,
dreaming wondrous roasted flavor,
and again find suety blankness.

The image of the living lamb
springs to mind, its dense marrow
churning out cells in hidden chambers
never expecting the light of day.
My stomach quails and I decide
not to swallow the bland mess,
but spit it in the sink,
rinse my mouth and get
some bittersweet chocolate
to forget.

Bird of Prey

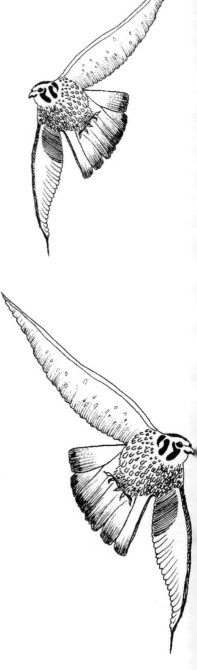

A dun midsized bird perched
on the top limb of a bush
watches.

Nondescript, neutral
like an oversized female robin,
for a long time it holds still
as if interested in nothing.

Then without warning
it leaps into the air, become
a kestrel in full flight,
crosshatched under-pattern
hypnotizing,
stunning net of death
falling on a dazzled mouse
whose last glimpse is
the swoop of that rapturing glory,
whose last sound heard is
the crack of her own neckbones.

Manet's Still Life With Fish

A large bass lies
on its left side,
tail laterally erect
like a frozen flag,
eye staring upward
facing lemon and a knife, unseen
facts in front of its snout,
but fixed sidelong by the smaller
flanking redfish, dead
but still frightened,
the oyster eyes far left,
blind but beseeching,
the eel, not accepting its fate,
crawling away.

Fish Monger

Tall
 and
  thin
   carrying
  his body
curved
  like a fishback
    you'd suspect
   him of
 fins
 rather
  than
     feet.
       Whistling
        he glides
         among
          his
         fishes
        smiling
     and clear eyes
   winking oval scales
  smile back. He loves
  them and even now
  cleaned and cased
    they can't help
       loving
        him.

Fisherman

I catch a fish
whose glistening eye,
is fixed upon immensity
invisible to me, sad fisherman

tied to what I eat,
transformed no further
by this hook and line
than by any thought of mine.

I am assigned to eat this fish,
wipe clean my dish and
wander the waters again
in hope to catch another—

perhaps to find, eating him,
I'll never get hungry again,
seeing with that fish's eye
the far side of immensity.

Spider

Huge and black in the web,
abdomen ten times her head,
forelegs weave, rear legs grip
and the small dun moth
surges in orbit but goes nowhere.

She looks as if slave bootblacks
toil in the dryrot
where she lies cool
through the day's heat,
rubbing her hide to gloss.

Often I've seen stilled
prey tacked up
seasoning on strands
stippled with morning dew
as the Queen awaits night.

Then to dine, solitary
but festive, anticipating
myriad spiderlets bred.
Caught in my thoughts,
I've shrugged and walked on.

But this modest moth,
beating against fate,
snares me so tightly
I cannot turn away
and leave it to die.

My hand parts the web.
The moth binds to me
by spider silk I pick away until
wings crumble, dull body
tumbles into matching duff.

Not a flicker of gratitude,
but what did I expect?
No witness to my deed
save the Queen.
Her many angry eyes

track my hand lifting the newspaper,
chill my spine as I read of
tragedies I can't remedy,
freeze my laughter at the comics.
Tomorrow, spun whole again,

the web will bind a fresh fly,
buzzing life wrapped for transfer.
I'll pass, and she won't even glance,
knowing my only choice: blunder on
into the web that is my life.

Part 5

Adventures, Misadventures

Dead of Winter

Nothing moves this winter night.
The door is bolted tight,
and every want and wish
buried deep in bedclothes.

My hawk of inspiration
flies over the land seeking
image, story, incantation,
but even to that keen vision
all fields are bare or fallow,
every creature in its hole.

No quarry, no chase.
A dead leaf scutters
along the pavement,
down the dark street.

Katusha

We had a cat,
Katusha,
freedom fighter
who'd come home torn raw,
a tom so ferocious
no consideration ever
made him see reason.

Human, he would have been
loner, assassin, victim—
still tiger but inept and
unfathomably lonely.
Bogart perhaps,
dragging on a coffin nail
as Bergman watched him turn away
or James Dean,
Natalie sensing
the crash already
ripped red behind his eyes
or Arthur Koestler
walking down the long hall
waiting for the bullet,
a woman's face
last in his mind.

Once, gone for weeks,
Katusha limped home
to be nursed, heal
and stalk the streets again.
Then, he never came back.
Caught, Father said

and like all the strays
sold for dissection.
Mother turned away.

Katusha, I can't forget
your yellow suicidal stare,
torn-up ears,
wailing in the dark.

Some nights
a boy still waits
for you, wild cat.
Come back!

Unhappy Dog

My dog sighs
not knowing why
I waste the day
typing lies
when he and I could
roam the earth
kicking dirt,
bellies arched in ecstasy.

I try to explain (in vain)
that I too am a dog
hot on a scent,
on one goal intent:
to feed my soul—
bone, old meat, or best
wild game within
tamed by my teeth.

Mouse stirs by the fence.
Footfalls brisk my ear.
Prick, freeze and point:
it rushes out, runs about.
I strike and snap,
break its back.
Blood bliss on my muzzle.
Howl thanks to the moon.

My dog is quizzical,
one ear up, the other down.
OK, he seems to say,
you can hunt
and even catch shadows
to feed your *soul*

(whatever that is, I don't know)—
we're two of a kind, if you will.
That's why I mind
this clickety-clack
till every treat has found its feet
and run into its hole—Oh,
I don't understand you at all!

Get up, get up, there's game afoot!
Life should be wild, my Master Hound—
snap to your feet, let's bound:
There is no dream inside of you
the wide world cannot make come true.

The Walk

He might as well be vegetable,
a limp bunch of celery,
rain-soaked road kill,
a dog-skin rug

for all the life he shows
sleeping the day through
until longer shadows trigger
some hormonal havoc.

Then up he jumps,
to speed around the room
and climb me like a tree
with taunting squirrel atop.

Now this dog, who lay
heavy as a hog in mud,
is lighter than a springbok,
energized to run the world,

bring to justice any
trespassed bird or cat,
savage any other dog
so foolish as to glance at me.

Suddenly my dog has eyes so dark,
so fevered when they fix on mine
and search the tissue of my brain,
I too begin to flare and pulse

and cannot find a single thought
within my fevered mind,
just the bite of surging blood,
the joy of hunting side by side.

Dog's New World

A gate opened where never before.
How could you resist the lure
of fresh terrain beneath a full moon?
A continent to be explored

and soon you had claimed it all.
No one challenged: you were King,
but trapped beyond a thorn-laced hill
so steep and sharp you fell back

torn and baffled each attempt,
until you limped the next-door patio
so sure you'd not see home again,
or so ashamed, you slunk away

when we came, as if we were strangers,
and cowered by the far wall.
The long hours spent lost
filled an ocean you could not cross,

home too big a notion for your brain.
Yet here you are again, in your own bed
transported by kind gods, your nightmare
fading fast as had the dream of home

when you found your new world
brightlit by the moon's shining eye
and felt yourself so solid in that land
until the eye clouded and darkness began.

Frogs

In Canada I caught two bullfrogs
netted in the dark night,
pulled from sweet wet freedom,
lunging for the solace of their swamp.

In Bio lab we'd started dissection
for which these frogs were destined:
pithed, to lie remote and squelchy,
powerful quadriceps limp.

I would slit them ventrally,
expose their organs' glistening colors,
liver and gall, brown and green,
red heart like a clenching fist.

That was how you learned, Dad said:
take things apart, see how they work.
I wanted to know as much as him,
how each organ spoke to every other.

But my frogs were magnificent!
Unlike the dwarves in Bio Lab,
these you could saddle and ride.
I gave them names and stories:

Sir Bounciful and Lady Hopforth,
waylaid by an evil sorcerer
who cast a spell on the Great Swamp.
This wizard, a mad scientist too,

instead of dissecting them swore
to change them into human friends
in trade for a lifetime's devotion,
doing precisely what he asked

no matter how wild his notions.
Once they proved loyal he'd let them
return to their native country,
there to sing praises of his name.

Meanwhile, they lived in a shoebox cell
lined with swampgrass from their home,
its lid tied down with string, until
left in the car during lunch

they baked in the summer sun.
The sorcerer mourned his friends,
missed them a day and then persisted
on his lonely way, seeking knowledge.

Dark Horse

Duchamp-Villier's black-patina'd
bronze-geared horse
grinds in brutal motion,
no nymph to tree
but warm blood to machine.

It is 1914, everything
driven, shattered—
horse become tank.

Crayfish

In a rainbarrel in the alley
lived three crayfish, content
in their utter strangeness,
but a child couldn't bear it
and had to interfere.

With their stalk eyes
and gray too-many legs,
did they see the baseball bat
descending calm and curious
until it chose one and pressed
lightly as it could
but too hard not to express
dark murk. Camouflage
or ruptured innards?

The child never knew which.
He jumped back, ran away,
and ever after
shied from strangeness.

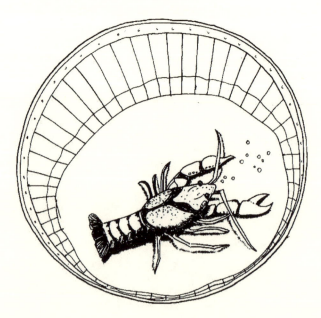

Never Say Die

Raccoons scream in the backyard,
fighting, mating, whatever their business
and our dog whines groans claws
at the door, fierce to wipe anything

not-dog from the gaping planet.
I remember when I was young
someone opened the door and boys
went with blood high shooting through

green vistas at the screaming enemy
caught in his own throes and not—
at first shock—shooting back.
Later, the flood tide of steel shat-

tered the air with screams of a new
meaning, and some came limping
home, pain bitten into their faces,
astonished that so small a people, so

small a place could ravage them through.
Some nights ago our dog caught
the raccoons, outweighed each three
to one but limped home torn bloody

about the ears eyes muzzle
with no evidence in the gray
morning light that any raccoon
was damaged or even fazed.

Nearly healed now he's ready
to go again, his young crazy
male heart hormonally mad
to defend to kill to be maimed

for his pack his tribe his kin,
for what if he could speak
he'd call his country.
He doesn't know he'll never learn

those raccoons are welcome
to the damned backyard all night
so long as he comes home alive
and sound as so many never did.

When I pull him from the door he
whimpers wild with pain of staying:
let me go die for you, let me go.
In the cozy light of our kitchen

suddenly between two breaths
I feel the world tilt
and my heart freezes over
white with fear for the future.

Encounter

The doe, dignified by motherhood,
has no sense of humor, but the crow
cannot stop laughing as his razor eye
watches curiosity lead the fawn
by its tentative nose to explore strangeness
in a wild turkey flock strutting like
Zulu warriors advancing on the drum beat
until the fawn breaks for Mother's teat,
large-eyed with surmise as the turkeys,
bereft of their target, rage at each other,
pecking and breasting former allies.

The crow preens his black purity,
glints behind spread flight feathers,
sums it up with one derisive squawk
and wings away to witness some new folly.

Spoiled Pet

Mighty rabbit, boss bunny
nosing out everything,
curiosity a cat's squared,
quizzical-eared
you want to know
want to own
every object on your run
that goes wherever I go.

Sweet insistent bunny,
nose twitching with inquiry,
white tail puff
marking your wisdom's progress,
I've felt no joy more pure
than yours in knowing motion,
simply bounding and finding.

Of skinned and stewing comrades
you know nothing
and though you feel so fiercely
entitled to know everything
(by virtue of profound rabbitude),
from that knowledge I'll defend you.
Lucky you. Who will defend me?

Part 6

Death Leaves His Card

Intimations

A curious, elfin animal,
catlike but unknown to science,
with tiny retractable claws,
has gotten into my chest.
Without haste or malice,
speculatively,
the creature rests its paw on my heart,
extends its nails and, lightly,
grips.

A shuddering lurch.
The heart spurts
a globed bloodball.
A dark veil falls.
The animal jumps back,
pads off to hide in a distant vein.

The heart regains its normal beat
but still oozes
from tiny clawpricks,
remembers the pain
and expects one day
the guest will return,
surround with careful teeth,
clamp, tear, and carry away.

Fool's Luck

Tremendous crackling in the branches:
wild turkey, tail askew, teeters on a limb
barely thick enough to hold it, maybe not—
so precarious yet so certain,
pompous and riotous as a clown,
blind to the coyote's tracking eye.

Stuttering cries: another heaves into sight,
ungainly mate or brother crashing on
the same encumbered route one wing-
beat from disaster but somehow rising
to tear through the woods' net
and come safe home.

A Hero of My Childhood

The orange tabby tomcat
running flat out
nearly made it
across the street
but the far front wheel
caught its tail
and, tethered,
it was forced to turn
belly up

and fight the tire,
there was nothing else—
slashing with back paws
until they went under
ripping with forepaws
until they went under
biting with teeth
until its head went under
screaming
screaming
screaming
until squashed flat

but still posed for combat
(face frozen, snarling,
claws frozen, out)
even broken
on the wheel.

A Dog I Knew

Lumps
should have been your nickname
for you grew them as the soil grows fruit,
abundant, various to touch and sight,
soft and mashable, hard and conical,
regions between. Predictably
one pitbull of a lump
locked its jaws around your throat
and would not loosen
before it squeezed out your life.

Where Did Joe Go?

Dad's crusty old mechanic
kept a huge Doberman
who tossed a 16-pound bowling ball
from wall to wall like balsa wood.

"Those jigaboos are scared shitless
of this dog," Joe grinned, "they don't
come near the garage while he's here."
The dog flung his toy, growled,
and genially thrust his head
beneath the grease-stained hand.

Joe's face showed sorrow,
a flicker of shame, then nothing.

Hand dead on the dog's head,
he'd disappeared—
remembering, Dad later said,
his son, killed at eighteen
by a drunken Black kid
who ran a light.

Was he mourning or murdering
back there in the dark of his mind?
He was gone, that's all we knew.

The Doberman slipped Joe's hand,
slouched away and sank into a corner,
black dog curled around a black ball.

Two Mice

Cat caught one.
Boy watched him
bat it around
the coal bin,
oh lovely glee,
eat it finally
head first,
wondrous
delicate bones
crunching,
tail fighting
engulfment
to the end,
twitching
counter-
clockwise.

Forty years later
another
whiskers unseen
along walls,
darts darkly
past dogs,
the proven path
to bird seed,
finds a new treat,
smells delicious,
nibbles
carefully
but

Snap.

No cat-
and-mouse,
no time-
tugged tail.
A domestic death
and then sealed
in a plastic bag.

Life Goes On

Our front hall runs from a gate
up stairs through a tunnel
to a dead end at the door
where spiders build webs
and wait for rising air
to bring prey.

One day a gangling cranefly
fumbled through the air and
got stuck on a silk lanyard
anchored to the wall by one end
and a branch at midstrand.
The cranefly threshed, whirled,

arced six inches from the wall,
only to be dragged back
by its leash's heft and spring.
Where the strand joined the wall
a gray spider waited, delicate,
a fifth its struggling captive's size.

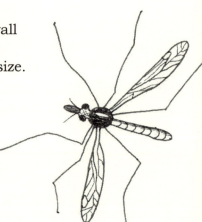

One lacy cranefly wing
bent painfully, and the long
elegant abdomen quivered.
Again and again it tried
and failed to change its fate.
The hunter held still.

On the ceiling, a dozen
larger, darker spiders rested
in their webs, unmoving, alert.

I turned away
from the hopeless cranefly
spent against the wall,

went in for breakfast
but could not eat, returned
with a flashlight to witness.
Light touching the cranefly
drove it into frenzy,
flying out and banging back

while the spider tensed,
testing its strand
with a skillful foreleg.
I moved before I knew it—
flicked my wrist and
broke the cranefly free.

Half tumbling half flying it crossed
the threshold, lost in our house.
The spider ran up its strand
and stopped as if shocked
by my brazen action.
Its dazed stillness said

that saving one victim
had merely made another.
I took a broom to the walls,
the ceiling, and swept away
that whole world.
Soon, the hall will fill again.

Glue Trap

Late at night
under the TV table
in flickering light,
a black streak.
Imagined?
No—again,
the other way,
dark sine wave.

Set the trap, Duty,
Pose the dream, Hope—
he's too quick
for greed to catch.

Morning light:
stuck, still,
reproaching.

Eyes fixed,
whiskers fine,
ears backlit,
tiny paws
clutched.

I know
my turn
will come.

How It Is

You'd think they'd know how,
canary parents:
bumbling about raising two young
huddled in the nest
barely breathing
except when it's time to eat.

So haphazard, instinct that
should be sure:
parents mating in the midst
of mothering, for there is no
fathering. Yet he helps,
puking food into her beak
that she stuffs into theirs
even as he screws her again.

It's incredible that any young
ever grow up. Some do end as
puddles on the cage floor
miserably dead, ignored—
but some do
yes
feather, fledge, and fly.

Part 7

Through a Glass Darkly

Bird Forms

                                                    S   K   Y
Gray   *whee*
                cart   ling   the
        bird   a   *ss*
                                            cro

            bird
Black
                tum*bl*   S   *m*
                    ing   the   r
                    th*rough*   t
                                                    o

Owl

I missed the place: got there late
and pulled in bladder-stricken
to find our flock of birders
peering out over the marsh.
"Go in the pole-barn," the guide said,
"The far end by the road
or the nesting owl will freak."

Back tensed, I watered a coyote bush,
expecting talons and the rending beak,
but finished, turned, and raised my field glasses
without ambush. The great-horned owl,
its body more shadow than shape,
like dark flames rising off brush,
stared down from her nest, huge
eyes lit from within glinting yellow.
I was stunned—she, indifferent
so long as I stayed away.

Snakes

Tiresias of Greek myth
separated coupling snakes,
became a woman; years later,
the same—became a man again.

Tiresias strikes them apart:
his groin boils over
and his prick rolls up
like a New Year's teaser.
The eruption leaves him
cratered.

His exploring hand
feels the ripe crescent
moon in his crotch.
He gets swacked
hits the town hard
wakes up with a man.

Would you believe
he splits them again?
His prick springs out
like a troll's tongue,
thwacks his nuts
and doubles him up.

Hera lugs him away
like an old suitcase
and springs the question
hoping to flatter Zeus—
which sex flies higher?
Women, oh my Queen!
She spits in his eye

rendering him blind
but Zeus prefers the truth
and makes him prophesy.
He crawls all over seeking
answers, finds another pair,
but can't get them apart.

Menzies' Wallflower

Four-petaled, mustard bright,
it lives sheltered among dunes
on the gray California coast
and nowhere else on earth:
lives in such sparse numbers,
to save it from browsing deer
it is jailed in small wire cages.

Seeking tongues stick in,
curl between thick wires,
lick the fleeting odor
whisked away by sea wind.
Will the last wallflower
eaten by the last deer
be the sweetest ever?

May that deer never know.
So vibrant breeding yellow
is Menzies' small wallflower,
even imprisoned let it multiply,
spreading like small suns until
it grips and holds whole beaches
and the gray dunes turn gold.

Sympathetic Magic

Your loathing of ants, Dear,

fear their crawling legs
will bring more crawling:

one ant appears, a scout,
finds a spot of food
and calls its fellows out

until there's a platoon
foraging and finding and then
putting out the word to come
again

which draws a horde,
traversing counters and drawers,
climbing toilet seats and doors,
searching every space that might provide
food of any kind, marching in and on—

I think you saw our house
drowned in seething ants top
to bottom, wrenched apart
piecemeal and carried away.
I told you they wanted only to be
fed and dry, but you freaked,

almost stamped your feet
at my fondness for these nameless
strivers, creatures I befriended
as a boy and confide in now
(they don't complain)—
chatting, arguing philosophy, un-
burdening myself of love and pain.

Cancer, you know, behaves much as you
conceive ants—opportunist first to last.
A scout comes—stealthy, alone—
whose messages of glee
at finding food for the colony
bring recruits in growing numbers
to search the distant corners
and overwhelm the occupants,

carry off the sources of their lives.
I wonder if your fear of multiplying
things foreshadowed your cancer,
revealed some hidden knowledge
of that growing sphere of cells
recruiting in your breast—or invited them?
Did sympathetic magic,
more powerful because unrealized,
steal away your body unaware?

Anemone

Stick your finger in.
It sucks gently
as if to greet you.

You may feel
you are welcome there
within that flexing grip.

Your fingertip dwells
in a close, wet cave
laved with sea.

You will not want to leave,
such comfort is this shelter
but the rest of you will tire.

The rest of you will require
as it always does
that you resume motion.

Pull your finger out.
The anemone relaxes, oozes
as if to clean you away.

Does the anemone welcome
penetration, like a ready woman,
or does it want to push out

the invader, like a woman taken
unwanting or before time?
Or does it merely crave

food of another kind?
If it were big enough,
or you small enough

Would it take you all in,
squeeze you all out,
hold and digest you?

Or would you gestate
in its inwardness,
emerge a new creature,

merman or mermaid,
or baby anemone fastened
to a gray shelter rock

to live there at peace,
caressing the occasional finger,
as the tide rolls in and out?

Some God or Other

The cat sits by the fire
curled up and watching,
sharp green eyes
annihilating
whatever they see.

In a moment or an hour
it will shift its long gaze
to me.

Handling the Ant

Roll it into a ball.
Can you feel
the black abdominal sac
pulse minutely
against your thumb?
Nothing will stop the antennae
waving and crinkling,
barely tickling your skin,
save pulling them off.

You can think, now,
it's just an ant
and squeeze
your thumb and index finger
until you feel the tiny pop.

Or you can think
my fingers hold a life,
see through insect eyes
the vast alien vise,
struggle in your own grip,
think
there might be me,
let the creature down
and watch it find
its old path.

Do just this
and save us all!

Part 8

How It Is

Just the Facts

Two

    fat black crows

        glance sidelong

            at the dog

        not intimidated

      not intimidating

    just stating

Here we are

Because They Know We Can't

Two birds explode into flight,
one chasing the other racing
nearly through my forehead,
barely swerving to miss as if
I were a mere pole or bush,
ground-stuck, of no account,
then skirt the hedge tops
rising dipping chittering madly
gladly till at last, out of sight
behind the farthest fence,
they perch, slanting their beaks,
shifting their laughing eyes.

Dry Winter

A solitary vireo bathes
in the dog's waterdish
while cedar waxwings
crash drunkenly among
redripe catonia aster berries.

Fall will not give in to winter
and these California birds
rejoice in the rainless season.
They know nothing
of cold and killing snow

but the Easterner in me tightens
waiting for the inevitable
blueglinting steel to fall.
The vireo hops to the bowlrim,
flicks me a bright glance,

appraises the wintry terrier
softly snarling at my side
and takes off just high enough
to evade the late-leaping dog,
the jaws' quick snap.

In their tree the vireo and a robin
so fat his breast nearly bursts
with color, sit slyly laughing
as the mongrel slouches off
to sleep and dream of wings.

You must accept they are laughing
even if you don't believe birds can
because their heads take a jaunty angle,
eyes glint and shift, tailfeathers lift,
subtle beaks smile, one time, two.

They laugh at the dog, more at his master
long since delivered from cold,
who won't accept this good fortune
but keeps a winter leashed within
to loose if this fine weather does not end.

Bipolar Order

At the Anchorage Zoo
two huge animals
both called *bear* but
different as man and wife
share an enclosure:
one Brown the other Polar
(Laurel and Hardy,
Vladimir and Estragon).

Sullen Brown sits on a ridge,
shaggy, studious hump,
worried something is not right,
moving only to avoid
his frolicking Polar opposite,
puppylike in slack white robe,
who romps as if oblivious
of bars, fence, faces,
topples bellyside up
down the watercourse,
juggles his ball alone, and
welcomes his captors' kindness.

At last he hauls white hide,
black snout from the water
to the bank, then the ridge,
and nudges his philosophic friend:
"No matter, come play!" But Brown
stiffens, broody with strain
to wrap his labored brain
around their dire situation.

Polar shrugs, inquires
one last time
over his shoulder,
but getting no reply
whacks his ball into the water,
sighs lightly, and follows after.

Mice in Winter

Nesting in our picnic basket
you ate forgotten peanuts
left over from some baseball game,
with brood of four swaddled
in the hall closet, snug among
Ace wraps and tampon shreds,
cloistered beneath coats with pockets
tracelessly pillaged for tidbits.

Like an undiscovered pygmy tribe
you lived your tiny secret lives
in a parallel and happy dimension,
until a foolish kit rustling shells
alerted the keen-eared housewife.
Then your peace was torn away.

Dark and startling, you popped up
twelve times your height and shot about
like hummingbirds cross-bred with roaches,
motoring among the hill-high dancing feet
and lunging cookpots improvised to traps
whose atonal clang celebrated your escape.

Soundlessly you pivoted and sparked,
then shot away faster than sight,
taking the germs you were to spread,
leaving the urinous odor of your lives
and sad departure settled on the walls.
However inspiring your flight,
home was lost, and outside, cold night.

Ant Morning

Solitary black ant, you explored the bathroom
day after day, crossing the glacier of the tub
as I brushed teeth three times your height.
Did you wander these wastes all night,
seeking some shred—gob, drop, flake—
to bring home for your kin? I will never
see with your eyes or feel with your legs or
understand what it means to live your life,
so close to nothingness, so filled
with the immensity of everything.

This morning when you were not there
I'd lost much more than you, solitary ant.

Elegy for Beauregard

1

Open the door and feel it—
whirling terrier rush of joy.
Worst, that instant of certainty
when hope flares only to go out.

My friend Regina says such ghosts
comfort: they mean the spirit lives.
Her English terrier,
ashes in a vase by the fireplace,
still jumps into bed at night
as always.

I think she's nuts.
Spiteful, these mirages,
nothing more,
melting nests of wasps
to sting your heart—
and this spirit business?
A placebo for cancer.

Perhaps because she lost
in the ovens of the dark land
so many she imagines
loving without reserve
(never having known them)
for her it comes easily,
to think the presence of the dead
friendly.

But I have never lost anyone
I'd admit to loving
without hating
except this small dog.

2

You came at age two
already named Beau
or was it Boo—the writing
was sloppy on the adoption paper.
But I knew you should be Beauregard,
handsome one whose bedroom eyes
enticed a treat, a walk, a butt-rub
no matter how tired I was.
You sat regally erect,
ears on permanent alert,
white diamond on your chest,
Prince Beauregard.

You had flaws,
but secret, nurtured apart
from the general gaze
or casual caress.
Felt closely, odd cones
dense as bones
studded your head,
samples of the varied lumps
your body grew, each original as you.

For so long all were benign,
nothing to cause worry
vets would say—
but they reminded me

of what one day would be,
the flaw that let in death.
Sometimes I wanted them cut out
as if that could help.
Now, sharp beneath my fingers
as your breath stops,
these malpositioned nipples
(on your belly were none)
are my last sense of you.

Scratch behind your ears
in those final days
and you rumbled
like a giant cat.
We thought it was pleasure,
our charming cat-dog,
not that lump turned traitor
wolfing your thyroid—
cruel choke collar
tightening.

3

I can't get rid of it,
this sense you are waiting
when I come home—
held back by an unseen leash,
some thing commanding *stay*
louder than I can wish *come.*

The forbidden rooms
are least lonely because
you were never there
so neither is the vacancy you left.

You would run
halfway, two-thirds up the stairs,
knowing the second story was
out of bounds but unable to resist,
afraid we'd miss the evening walk.
As I climb the stairs now
you fade. Turn the corner at the top
and I am safe from haunting.
But I can't come down.

You were my guide, my master.
You taught me how to breathe,
to rejoice, and now
to grieve.

4

"Dog with chocolate ears," Kathy said
as they brought the sedative
before they took you in
for the final shot.
And I had to scream "Stop!
Don't you know," I couldn't say,
"you're tearing strips off me?"

5

You were so patient,
sitting still far longer
for your portrait
than most dogs would,
wanting to be free
but sensing what we wanted
and giving it.

"Stay," we'd command, and you'd give
a puzzled look that said
"if you insist, but whatever for?"
Now, if it would work, we'd shout
"Come," but your picture rightly
would return that quizzical look.

                    6

You hated your own kind,
attacked every other dog,
friendly or not, remembering perhaps
when we beat off three setters
who mugged you at the beach.
You cowered beneath your leash
and I'll bet vowed *never again*,
for then began your anti-dog crusade.

It's so hard to think of you
as anything but knowing,
deciding in a conscious way,
even if your every act
was simply adaptation.
Worthless at fetch unless
the thrown thing was edible,
you'd glance sidelong, eloquent
with suspicion, saying "if you won't
chase that ball why should I?
And bring it? Come on!"

But your paws were all white
on brown, soft-furred legs:
"Little booties, four white booties,"
the old lady crooned as if to a baby
as you passed without interest,

ear cocked vaguely, wondering
why the fuss.

In the *tonglen* technique,
Buddhists take in the world's grief,
transform it to love
and send it out again.
You had your own way:
your ears, straight up
(natural or cropped no one knew)
like the spine in yoga,
were swiveling radar screens
that took in grief and everything else
and sent out attitude.

7

So many memories:
Your crazy-ass crooked tail,
a lateral question mark
hooked left and refusing,
stubborn as your terrier brain,
any attempt to straighten.
Beard edged with dogfood
you rubbed off on the couch,
wiry hair sprung like a Mohawk
all along your spine.
Only fire and the Vet scared you.
Lead you before a cozy hearth
or in for a routine check
and you became
a trembling, drooling mess.

The German woman at the kennel
said "Ziss dogk hass a screw loose,
und not chust lately—he vaz born zat vay"

and when we came to bring you home
you'd become Screwloose Lautrec,
unhinged, crazy-dog expressionist,
painting leaps and spins in air,
Kandinsky orbits of delight.

"What kind of dog is that?"
people wondered as we passed
so often that we made up a breed,
Tasmanian Goat Hound:

the one who broke the mold,
who was only himself,
but also everything else—
cat-dog, fish-dog, devil,
wild-haired rocker,
the one who came,
the one who wouldn't,
the one who insisted,
the one who is gone.

8

The silence is so oppressive
not because there is no sound
but because it doesn't include *your* silence.
Your presence has become an absence,
that absence again a presence
that eats away everything, like acid,
and leaves an empty, smoking hole.

9

Young, fresh from that first
Nazi master or mistress,
you feared nearly everything,
cringed your way through life,

but then were born again,
borrowing our confidence
(or fear), and began to lunge
at whatever moved—dog, cat, human—
until, grown old, you knew it all belonged
and could be trusted, so you changed
the lunge for the nuzzle.

10

Cramped by the walls
of the pricey heated bed
we bought for your arthritis,
you stuck with your stained blue cushion
and treated yourself by basking
nose-first in the wall-vent's hot stream.
Now you've escaped any constraint,
and lie perhaps alongside canis major,
with all Space in which to live your death,
but no heat in that utter chill.

Outside, deep fog drips like rain,
the San Francisco murk
you plowed like a boat through spray,
happy to be cool
and fastened to the scent,
towing me behind.

How can I find a hold
against this grief
sucking me away?
Feel the riptide
and dare to tell me
this was *only* a dog!

Unable to stop loving,
even certain you are nowhere
I must imagine you somewhere—
crazy hair stirring in the wind,
following your nose
up your favorite trail
and off into the trees.
I believe in nothing
I have not witnessed
yet I seem to have no choice
than believe in you.

Changelings

Perhaps five, the wild-haired boy
flushed with sun and wind
runs shrieking with laughter
round and round the picnic table,
plump younger sister stumbling
giggling after, reaching for the
drumstick held just out of reach.
Their smiles and their parents'
intersect to make a globe of warmth
that glows around them.

Outside that shimmering shell
of sun and sand and wind and joy
I try to glow too as I walk by,
to join their family by pantomime,
smiling and nodding as if I know.

But I am ignorant of life like theirs,
my pretense like a sucked-out egg
painted and lacquered for show
but at the center, hollow. There
I cradle my never-born child,
the empty space in the bulb
of a cast-up kelp.

I am sorry
my stalwart son
my lovely daughter
that you were orphaned
before you could be born.

But the sea rolls up to the shore
holding out two otters in its arms.

Tourist

Outside our train, Alaska passes huge:
cloudframed mountains insistent white,
closer aspen's golden rivers
flooding deepgreen spruce.
With calf, a mother moose flees,

casting over her shoulder
a glance of reproach.
I try to think my thoughts,
feel feelings of beauty, ecstasy.
Instead, a whack on my knee.

He can't be more than four,
this darkhaired, broadfaced boy
racing up and down the aisle
that is to him perhaps
horsetrack, dragstrip, spaceship.

More real to him his inner world
than the outsized grandeur
rushing past windows hard
to see from even standing on a seat.
Lost behind his face, reflected

back more fascinating every moment,
he smiles to find himself safe against
the strange world, palms flat on the cold pane,
and marvels at his bracketing prints,
squealing at so fine a thing, him.

Now he's down again, off to his races,
but this time I catch him as he hurtles
past, throbbing body, and hold.
I've tapped into a dynamo: electric
juice bubbles through my hands.

His head turns slowly and he looks
through me as if I were Alaska,
very large but irrelevant.
Please don't bump into me, I say.
I smile, and he studies my face

wonderingly, as I would a landscape.
He smiles back, some recognition made.
Look for a moose, I say, making antlers
of my arms and hands. He nods,
large-eyed, backs, and spins off.

I turn to the window and see a waterfall
diving silver down three hundred feet.
Pulled from myself, newborn from mother,
I feel beauty's cold sparkle on my skin,
spume of time sinking, not to come again.

Will that boy think of me in sixty years
when I am dead and he fondly
reaches for his early memories
to save of himself what he can,
to fix his print against the Cold?

Will he wonder why he remembers
my strange hands and face
among his parents', his aunties', his own?
Or will he know by then that he remembers
because this foretaste of awakening

was but the first in a lifetime when
the world would reach out and grip
amid his games and say *pay attention*
if you want to live. Dream on
and you'll never get off the train.

Will his memory be all that's left of me?
I have come to find the pitiless blue
at the core of glaciers, to be shrunk
by the uncaring bulk of mountains
and being small, to lose myself

in a rushing world that holds and drops me.
The love of mother moose for calf offers
safety amid tumult; the wild land
saturate with passing beauty
offers peace amid the riot of change.

I watch the boy's receding back.
He turns toward me again an old man
whose flake of memory is all I am—
one who kindly woke him to the world.
If that's what's left of me, let it be enough.

About the Author

Dan Liberthson has a PhD in English literature from the State University of New York at Buffalo. Born in Rochester, New York, he has made his home in San Francisco and the Bay Area since 1978. Dan has published widely in poetry journals and is the author of *A Family Album: Living With Schizophrenia (2006)*, a book of poems describing the joys and heartaches of growing up in a perfectionist Jewish immigrant family with a mentally ill sister. He has also published *The Pitch is on the Way: Poems About Baseball and Life* (2008; illustrated by Nicolette Ausschnitt), which celebrates his life-long love of baseball, including poems about every fielding position, the art of batting, and auxiliary personnel such as umpires, managers, and fans. For further information about Dan's poetry and to place orders for books, please visit his website, **Liberthson.com**.

About the Artist

Cassandra Mettling-Davis is a residential architect with her own practice in San Francisco, CMD Architecture. She graduated from the University of California at Berkeley after attending City College of San Francisco, where she completed coursework in drawing, painting, and architecture. A sixth-generation San Francisco native, Cassandra lives in Miraloma Park with her husband and cats, who refused to pose for any illustrations.

Made in the USA
Middletown, DE
09 July 2021

43778593R00085